W9-BOL-519

THE BATTLE OF IWO JIMA

Turning the Tide of War in the Pacific

BY STEVEN OTFINOSKI

Consultant:
Richard Bell, PhD
Associate Professor of History
University of Maryland, College Park

CAPSTONE PRESS
a capstone imprint

Tangled History is published by Capstone Press,
1710 Roe Crest Drive, North Mankato, Minnesota 56003
www.capstonepub.com

Library of Congress Cataloging-in-Publication Data
Names: Otfinoski, Steven, author.
Title: The Battle of Iwo Jima : turning the tide of war in the Pacific / by
Steven Otfinoski.
Description: North Mankato, Minnesota : Capstone Press, 2020. | Series:
Tangled history | Includes bibliographical references and index. | Audience:
Grades 4-6. | Audience: Ages 8-12.
Identifiers: LCCN 2019006033| ISBN 9781543572582 (hardcover) | ISBN
9781543575583 (pbk.) | ISBN 9781543572629 (ebook pdf)
Subjects: LCSH: Iwo Jima, Battle of, Japan, 1945—Juvenile literature.
Classification: LCC D767.99.I9 O84 2020 | DDC 940.54/2528—dc23
LC record available at https://lccn.loc.gov/2019006033

Editorial Credits
Christopher Harbo and Nick Healy, editors; Kazuko Collins, designer;
Eric Gohl, media researcher; Laura Manthe, production specialist

Photo Credits
Alamy: Archive Image, 92, Everett Collection Inc, 34, nsf, 18, 96, PJF
Military Collection, 31, 103, RBM Vintage Images, 21, 48, 50, 67, 105; AP
Photo: Ernest K. Bennett, 25, Joe Rosenthal, 62; Bridgeman Images: UIG/
Buyenlarge Archive, 32; Getty Images: Bettmann, 75, Louis R. Lowery,
101, PhotoQuest, 13, Stringer/JIJI PRESS, 37, Stringer/Keystone, 83, The
Asahi Shimbun, 29; Library of Congress: 44; National Archives and Records
Administration: cover, 7, 8, 17, 23, 27, 38, 43, 60, 68, 73, 80, 89, 91, 95;
Newscom: Everett Collection, 98, KRT/Lou Lowery, 47, Photoshot/War, 79;
Shutterstock: Peter Hermes Furian, 11; Wikimedia: Public Domain, 14, 55,
77, U.S. Navy, 4

Printed and bound in the United States of America.
PA70

TABLE OF CONTENTS

The Japanese attack on Pearl Harbor destroyed nearly 200 U.S. military aircraft and several battleships while taking more than 2,000 lives.

FOREWORD

The Japanese sneak attack on the U.S. naval base at Hawaii's Pearl Harbor on December 7, 1941, plunged the United States into World War II (1939–1945). For the next six months, the Japanese dominated the Pacific region. But after the U.S. won the Battle of Midway Island in June 1942, the tide began to turn. On land, sea, and in the air, U.S. forces began to take back Japanese-held islands in the South Pacific. They used them as stepping-stones to work their way toward their ultimate goal—mainland Japan.

One of the most critical of these stepping-stones was the tiny island of Iwo Jima. It was an unlikely prize. Meaning "sulfur island" in English, Iwo Jima was a barren, forbidding place, nearly devoid of plant and animal life. This eight-square-mile island was created by volcanic activity. Its main natural feature was the extinct volcano Mount Suribachi, 556 feet (70 meters) high, located at its southern tip. The Japanese set up a radar warning system to alert the mainland of approaching U.S. B-29 bomber planes. The island, located about 760 miles (1,220 kilometers) south of the Japanese capital of Tokyo, was also a key air base for Japanese bomber planes.

The Americans wanted to take Iwo Jima away from the Japanese. They wanted to use it as their own base for planes attacking the mainland. They could also use the island as an emergency landing field for larger aircraft needing to refuel or be repaired before or after bombing raids.

But taking Iwo Jima would not be easy. The island was honeycombed with natural caves and tunnels made from volcanic rock. In June 1944, the newly appointed commander of Japanese forces, General Tadamichi Kuribayashi, arrived on Iwo Jima. He had his men build many pillboxes—small, low concrete shelters for machine guns and other weapons. His soldiers also dug about 11 miles (18 km) of new tunnels and other underground fortifications to strengthen the island's defenses. This defensive system was largely hidden from view and blended into the barren, rocky landscape.

Also, beginning in June, U.S. planes and naval ships began heavily bombing the island, hoping to soften the Japanese defenses against a planned land invasion. It became the longest, most intense bombing pre-assault of any enemy site in the Pacific. But despite the bombing, the Japanese defenses were not seriously damaged.

By February 1945, the Americans prepared their land invasion. Three divisions of Marines,

U.S. Marines would face difficult terrain on the island of Iwo Jima, and the enemy's defenses would prove difficult to overcome.

numbering about 60,000 men and traveling from the U.S.-occupied Mariana Islands, would land on Iwo Jima. They were unaware of the ordeal that awaited them there.

1

U.S. Marines study a map of Iwo Jima while a ship carries them toward the small but strategically important island.

"I PRAY FOR A HEROIC FIGHT"

Captain Dave Severance

Hilo, Hawaii
Early February 1945

Captain Dave Severance walked from the Marine training grounds to his superior's headquarters with a feeling of dread. Lieutenant Colonel Chandler Johnson had a reputation for having a hot temper. Severance wondered if he had done something wrong to offend Johnson. Severance had done his best to be a good leader to the men of Company E, better known as Easy Company. His men seemed to like and respect him. Together they had been preparing for the invasion of Iwo Jima, only a few weeks away.

Severance marched into the command post and saluted Johnson, a heavyset man sitting behind his desk. Johnson did not look pleased to see him.

"Where is your company?" Johnson demanded.

"Back in the assembly area," Severance said. "I thought you wanted to see me alone."

Johnson's faced turned bright scarlet and his eyes flashed. "You are relieved of your command!" he bellowed.

As Severance stood there in shock, Johnson sent word to E Company's executive officer to bring the company forward. Receiving no further orders from Johnson, Severance did not know what to do. He trailed Johnson and his staff as they left the building.

Suddenly, the colonel turned to him in surprise. "What are you doing here, Dave?" he asked.

"You relieved me of my command, sir," was all he could think to say.

Johnson glared at him impatiently. "Get the hell back with your company!" he commanded.

Severance hurried away, shaking his head in disbelief. He was beginning to see that the colonel's temper could change as quickly as the weather on Iwo Jima.

General Tadamichi Kuribayashi

Iwo Jima
February 13, 1945, morning

General Tadamichi Kuribayashi nodded approvingly when he saw the concrete tunnel—one of many built by his soldiers since his arrival in June. He had overseen the building of a maze of interconnected tunnels and fortifications that

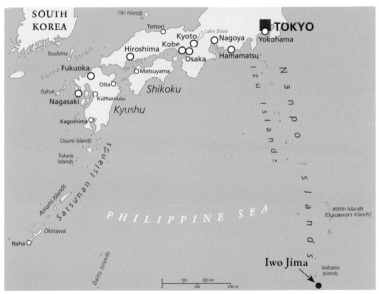

Located about 750 miles (1,200 km) south of Tokyo, Iwo Jima appears as a tiny speck on maps. Its location made the island's airfield important to U.S. plans to invade Japan and to Japan's efforts to turn back enemies.

supported the island's natural caves and tunnels. These fortifications had held up well under eight months of daily bombardment from U.S. fighter planes.

But the general knew there was worse to come. Japanese intelligence had learned of a massive land invasion the Americans had been planning for months. It could begin any day now.

Kuribayashi, a 30-year military veteran and a member of the samurai caste, had no illusions. It was all but inevitable that the island would fall to the Americans' superior forces. His goal was to hold off a U.S. victory as long as possible and inflict as much damage as he could. This could discourage the Americans from attacking the mainland and might even lead to a negotiated peace.

To accomplish this goal, Kuribayashi set a grim challenge for his men. They were expected to kill at least 10 Americans before each of them was killed. The fortifications they had built would help them live long enough to fulfill this vow.

Kuribayashi left the tunnel and returned to his headquarters. He sat down and wrote a letter to

Japanese General Tadamichi Kuribayashi led the defense of Iwo Jima.

his beloved wife, Yoshii. In previous letters, he had done his best to prepare her for what was to come. In one letter he wrote, "You must not expect my survival." This time he would not write about the grim future but instead try to remind Yoshii of happier days from their past.

General Holland Smith commanded two divisions of U.S. Marines in the attack on Iwo Jima.

General Holland Smith

General Holland Smith gazed out at the blue Pacific waters from the flagship *Eldorado*, bound for the island of Iwo Jima. His thoughts were on the two divisions of Marines under his command, now headed to the tiny island.

Smith was the top Marine in the Pacific theater of war and one of the most renowned. He had served bravely in France during World War I (1914–1918) and remained a fierce supporter of the Marine Corps.

Like Colonel Johnson, Smith had a temper. His nickname, "Howling Mad" Holland, was well earned. But, like Johnson, he could also turn from anger to laughter in a moment and had a lively sense of humor.

Little of that humor was displayed in his disagreements with his fellow commanding officers in the Navy. They had promised him three days of naval bombardment of Iwo Jima to soften up the enemy before the Marines landed. But Smith felt that was not enough. He had seen the fighting spirit of the Japanese soldiers up close on other island battlefields. He was convinced it would take more than three days of bombing to discourage them. He feared that the cost of Marine lives once they landed would be high. Then Smith walked back inside to meet with his host on the flagship, Vice Admiral Richmond Turner.

General Tadamichi Kuribayashi

His headquarters, Iwo Jima
February 15, 1945, late afternoon

All day General Kuribayashi had been receiving reports from his commanders of the U.S. ships approaching the island's southern tip. Ship after ship was sailing into the bay, much to the surprise of his aides. But the general remained cool and confident, at least on the outside.

On the inside, he too was concerned about the invaders. The night before he had sent a message by radio to the Imperial Navy, asking for more troops to help in the coming battle. The commanders replied that they would be able to send reinforcements, but not until April 1. That was six weeks away.

Kuribayashi seriously questioned if his men could hold out that long. But he refused to give in to negative thoughts. Not now, before the battle had even begun. He went to his microphone and spoke to his troops through the loudspeaker system.

"All shout 'Banzai' for the emperor!" he exclaimed. "I have the utmost confidence that you will do your best. I pray for a heroic fight."

U.S. Marines advance inland after a massive and at times chaotic landing that involved hundreds of watercraft carrying troops, vehicles, and weapons.

Mount Suribachi loomed in the distance during the U.S. invasion of Iwo Jima.

"BE READY TO GO IN FIVE MINUTES"

Joe Rosenthal

Aboard landing craft off Iwo Jima,
February 19, 1945, 7:30 a.m.

Joe Rosenthal held on to the side of the landing boat for dear life as it pounded against the churning waters. He took off his glasses and wiped the saltwater from them so he could see the approaching land. Poor eyesight had kept him from becoming a military photographer for the Army. His persistence, however, had earned him an assignment to cover the Pacific theater for the Associated Press news service.

Rosenthal had proven his worth as a war photographer in New Guinea, Guam, and other Pacific island battlefields. Now he was about to land on what could be his most important assignment of all—Iwo Jima.

Rosenthal looked around at the young Marines surrounding him on the deck. None of them looked out of his teens. At age 33, he imagined he was the oldest person on the boat. He wondered how many of these young men would die in the hours to come. He wondered if he himself would survive.

Usually a sociable person, Rosenthal was not in the mood to talk to the Marines. He did not want to know where they came from or whom they had left behind. He did not want to know and come to like men whom he might never see alive again.

As the boat drew closer, Rosenthal could see the island's highest point, Mount Suribachi. It rose out of the morning mist, an ugly, brown hump. It seemed to brood over Iwo Jima like some misshapen giant. He took it as a bad omen of things to come.

Private Ira Hayes

The beach at Iwo Jima
February 19, 1945, late morning

Private Ira Hayes waited tensely in the landing craft as it quickly approached the beach. Hayes was a member of Easy Company and one of the few

American Indians in the group. He was of the Pima tribe and grew up on the Gila River Reservation in Arizona in a one-room adobe house. He enlisted in the Marines at age 19 and took pride in his service. But now he was as scared as any of the Marines who stood around him.

Private Ira Hayes volunteered for training as a Marine paratrooper and graduated from Parachute Training School before he was deployed in the Pacific.

Their craft hit the beach hard and the ramp came down, releasing the men. Hayes jumped from the ramp and looked down and saw a dead Marine lying at the shoreline. His stomach churning, Hayes ran up the beach. The air was filled with the stench of gunpowder and blood.

Captain Dave Severance

The beach at Iwo Jima
February 19, 1945, late morning

Captain Severance braced himself as his landing craft reached the beach. As he and his men scrambled out onto the sand, he felt his feet sink down to his ankles. He remembered this was a volcanic island. The volcanic dust blended with the sand, turning it into a soft, squishy mix. He and the other Marines struggled to make their way through this mire. He felt like he was running in a bin of wheat. But the sound of gunfire and shellfire made him quicken his steps until he reached the prearranged assembly area, about 100 yards (91 m) in from the beach.

Company E did not have an honored role in the initial assault. Colonel Johnson had given that position to Companies D and F, which he felt were the most combat ready. Severance's company would serve in a reserve position.

The captain was pulled from his thoughts by a command to appear before the regiment

U.S. Marines inched forward in the volcanic sand on a slope near the beach where landing craft came ashore.

commander, Colonel Harry Liversedge. His post was a stone's throw from the assembly area.

Liversedge explained to him that officers expected a Japanese counterattack any time. He asked Severance if he was ready to move out.

"Our 2nd Platoon is still absent, Colonel," Severance replied.

Liversedge did not look pleased. "Be ready to go in five minutes or I'll give you a general court-martial!" he cried.

A responsible and able officer, Severance could not believe that he had again earned the anger of one of his superiors. He ran down the line looking for the 2nd Platoon. There was no sign of them. He decided not to draw the colonel's wrath again. He returned to the post and told Liversedge they were ready to move out. The colonel nodded curtly. But to Severance's great relief, the counterattack did not come. In a few minutes, the missing platoon joined them. He and his men were safe and had suffered no casualties . . . so far.

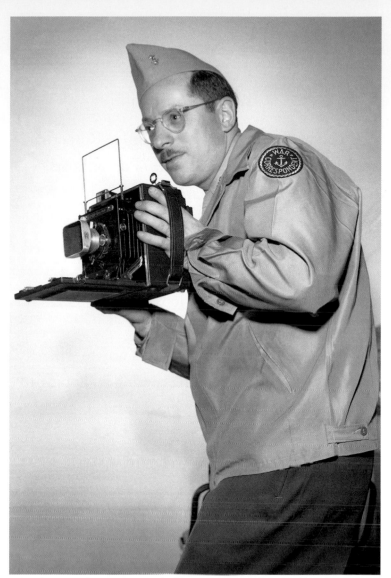

War photographer Joe Rosenthal's images from the island battle appeared in newspapers all across the United States.

Joe Rosenthal

It had been a long afternoon for Joe Rosenthal. After lining up with a multitude of other boats, his landing craft finally reached the beach about noon. He followed the Marines, rushing up the sand, dodging bullets and mortar fire. He snapped as many pictures as he could of the chaos and destruction. Everywhere he looked he saw dead Marines and body parts.

Now Rosenthal was making his way to where the reinforcement boats would be coming in, hoping to hitch a ride back to the flagship. He had one goal in mind, and it was not escaping from Japanese fire.

More important to him was getting his film ready to send off to Guam. There it would be developed and sent back to the United States for publication. These graphic photographs would show the Americans back home the fierce fighting that was happening on Iwo Jima. They would see the sacrifices the Marines were making for them.

General Holland Smith

Aboard the *Eldorado*
February 19, 1945, early evening

General Smith was perplexed. He had notified his commanders onshore to be prepared for a counterattack from the Japanese by nightfall. But hour after hour had passed and there was no sign of engagement from the enemy. The Japanese had fired

General Smith (left) and other U.S. commanders watched the amphibious assault from a ship near the island.

furiously earlier on the beach at the first assault, but since then had been silent.

Smith was more than frustrated. A counterattack would mean more casualties, but it would draw the enemy out of the caves and tunnels that protected them. The longer they remained safely out of sight, the longer it would take to seize the island. And the more Marines would die. The first day of the battle was not ending well, Smith decided. It looked as if they would be in for a long siege.

General Tadamichi Kuribayashi

Command Post, Iwo Jima
February 19, 1945, evening

General Kuribayashi received the reports of more and more Marines gathering on the beach with great satisfaction. He would wait until the shoreline was crowded with them before giving the order to attack again. The soldiers stationed atop Mount Suribachi would tell his commanders where to strike for the greatest advantage.

General Tadamichi Kuribayashi (second from left) studies a map while preparing the defense of Iwo Jima.

Kuribayashi had no use for the banzai attacks favored by some commanders. In these attacks, soldiers ran directly at the enemy in a frontal assault, waving swords and rifles. In many cases, they were cut down before they got close enough to do any harm to the enemy. It was a wasteful, worthless gesture he would not tolerate on Iwo Jima. It was much more effective to fire on the Americans from hidden strongholds. Only then would General

Kuribayashi gain the precious time that the Imperial forces needed to regroup on the mainland.

But there was one thing that Kuribayashi, for all his careful planning, had not counted on. He had not thought the Americans would die so readily for their cause. The hundreds of bodies that lay on the bloody beach testified to their commitment. They were willing to sacrifice themselves, just as his own men were. And there were many more Marines to take the place of those who fell in combat. A surplus of troops was an advantage that Kuribayashi did not enjoy.

Corporal Hershel "Woody" Williams

Aboard ship in harbor
February 20, 1945, 3 a.m.

Corporal Woody Williams did not scare easily, but now he was scared. After waiting hours on board his ship, he had to climb 50 feet (15 m) down a rope ladder in the dark to the deck of a landing craft. What scared him the most was the 60-pound

Corporal Hershel "Woody" Williams

(27-kilogram) backpack he was carrying. If he slipped from the rope and fell in the water, he knew he would drown, weighed down by the backpack. Besides that, he could not swim.

Williams made it into the landing craft, but remained there for the rest of the day. The beach was so crowded with Marines, there was no room for his outfit. They would have to stay put until some of the men moved off the beach. It seemed strange to be sitting there safe from harm while hundreds of fellow Marines were fighting on the beach. But there was nothing he could do but wait.

A U.S. torpedo bomber plane high above Iwo Jima

Lieutenant Colonel Chandler Johnson

American battle line, Iwo Jima
February 20, 1945, morning

It had been a hellish night for the Marines of the 2nd and 3rd Battalions. The Japanese had kept up a constant fire through the darkness, giving the men little time to rest or sleep.

Lieutenant Colonel Johnson, commander of the 2nd Battalion, was determined to boost his men's morale. Disregarding his own safety, he walked among the troops. He wore a fatigue cap on his head with a pistol jutting out of his right hip pocket. The men seemed to appreciate his visit. With the possibility of a long, drawn-out battle before them, they needed all the morale-boosting he could give them.

American troops aboard a landing craft approach the island of Iwo Jima.

"I WILL TRY AS HARD AS I CAN TO LIVE"

Corporal Woody Williams

Aboard ship approaching Iwo Jima
February 21, 1945, 3:30 a.m.

Corporal Williams watched tensely as the beach on Iwo Jima drew closer. All in all, it had been a frustrating 24 hours. After waiting all day to leave his landing craft, Williams and the other Marines had been taken back to the mother ship at 10 p.m. They were fed and went to bed. Then at 3 a.m. the process had started all over again. They were herded from the ship into amtracs, tractors that could travel through water.

Now with a jolt, Williams's amtrac lumbered up to the beach, where it became stuck in the slushy sand.

Williams clambered out of the amtrac with the other men and scrambled up the beach. The sand beneath his feet felt like a floor covered with BBs. Bullets whizzed around him. There was nowhere to run for cover. The only form of shelter was the holes in the ground made by fallen mortar shells. Each hole held as many as 10 soldiers, and the competition to get into one was fierce. Williams finally found a hole with some room and dove in.

Colonel Baron Takeichi Nishi

Command post, Iwo Jima
February 21, morning

Colonel Baron Takeichi Nishi listened to the American radio broadcast with some amusement. While U.S. propaganda tried to convince Japanese soldiers to surrender, this broadcast was aimed at an audience of just one. Him.

The announcer was pleading for him—Baron Nishi, as he was known—to surrender. There was good reason for this heartfelt appeal. Nishi was probably the most celebrated Japanese person on the island. Besides being a cavalry officer in the Imperial Army, he was also a celebrated equestrian.

Riding his beloved horse, Uranus, Nishi had won the gold medal in the individual jumping event

Baron Takeichi Nishi during the 1932 Olympic Games, which were held in the United States

at the 1932 Los Angeles Summer Olympics. The time he spent in California after the Olympics was among his most cherished memories. He had been befriended by many Hollywood celebrities. They admired not only his horsemanship, but also his bubbly personality and warm friendship.

But that was all before the war. Now the Americans and Japanese were sworn enemies. And

Nishi was the commander of the tanks that would attack the Americans landing on Iwo Jima.

Nishi had much in common with his commander. Like him, General Kuribayashi was a member of an old and distinguished family. Yet Nishi was not happy with the general's orders for his tanks. They would not be mobilized to attack

An American tank got stuck in the fine sand of Iwo Jima, which posed difficulties in the movement of U.S. military vehicles and troops.

the Americans but, like the soldiers, would be hidden from view. The tanks were literally buried, with only their turrets and guns aboveground. This, to Nishi, was not a way to fight a war. There was nothing heroic about it.

Heaving a sigh, he turned off the radio. He did not like fighting the Americans, but he would not surrender. He felt the piece of Uranus's mane that he carried in his pocket. He looked at it as a good luck charm. He would fight to the end and hope to survive. As he told family members before he left Tokyo for the last time, "I will try as hard as I can to live."

Captain Dave Severance

Command post, Iwo Jima
February 21, late morning

Waiting tensely for the order to move out, Captain Severance received a command that required only a few of his men. The tanks on the beach were ready to move inland. Men from Easy Company were needed to guide them up toward Mount Suribachi. Severance gave the job to three men in his 1st Platoon. Each man positioned himself in front of a tank and then guided the tank around mines, holes, and dead and wounded Japanese soldiers, urging the tank drivers on with hand signals. It was difficult work and Severance watched with pride as his men did their job.

Lieutenant Colonel Chandler Johnson

A hill near his command post
February 21, early afternoon

Lieutenant Colonel Johnson looked intently through his binoculars at the progress the tanks and foot soldiers were making. Hurling grenades and shooting flamethrowers, they were blowing up and burning out the Japanese soldiers hidden in their pillboxes. They were on the path that led to their ultimate goal—Mount Suribachi. He had misjudged Easy Company and its commander, Captain Severance. They were fighting with no less passion and skill than any other company of Marines on Iwo Jima.

Chomping on an unlit cigar, Johnson climbed down the hill. He soon caught up with the soldiers marching steadily forward. He patted one soldier on the shoulder.

"Son, you've won yourself the Navy Cross," Chandler said. "Hang on to command of that platoon."

With any luck, the colonel thought, by tomorrow they would be in a good position to start climbing the mountain. And the men of Easy Company, he decided, would be leading the charge.

Private Ira Hayes

Near Mount Suribachi
February 22, late afternoon

Private Hayes was a part of Easy Company's 2nd Platoon, which was now surrounding the base of Mount Suribachi. Word spread among the soldiers that tomorrow they would be heading up the mountain. They did not know how many enemy soldiers they would confront there, or if they would even make it to the summit alive.

The risk of death was very much on the mind of Hayes, but he dealt with it with his characteristic sense of humor. As soldiers gathered by the mountain, Hayes was forming little mounds of earth with his hands. One soldier commented that the mounds looked like fresh graves. Hayes mouthed a version of "Taps," the bugler's tune played at funerals. Then he said to one of his fellow soldiers, "This is just in case I'm not around when you get it."

The soldier glared at him and kicked over the mounds. Hayes just smiled.

An explosion on Mount Suribachi with U.S. troops looking on from the summit

"THE FLAG'S UP!"

U.S. Marines fight from behind cover on Iwo Jima with Mount Suribachi in the distance.

Captain Dave Severance

Southeastern end of the base of Mount Suribachi
February 23, 1945, early morning

Captain Severance's field telephone rang loudly. On the other end was Colonel Johnson. "Send me a platoon!" he ordered Severance.

Severance looked over his men. Four men from the 2nd Platoon, including Private Hayes, were exploring the base of the mountain. He chose the remaining members of the 3rd Platoon, the nearest to Johnson's command post, to report to the colonel. Severance knew what Johnson wanted them to do—climb the mountain. To give them a better fighting chance against the Japanese they would encounter, he added more men to the platoon, bringing the number to 40. He wished them well and sent them on their way.

Lieutenant Colonel Chandler Johnson

Command post
February 23, 9 a.m.

Lieutenant Colonel Johnson looked over the men of Easy Company's 3rd

Platoon. He knew these were brave men, some of whom might never return from their dangerous mission. Before sending them off, he turned to his adjutant and asked him to hand him the U.S. flag from his map case. Then he handed the flag to the platoon's leader, First Lieutenant Harold George Schrier.

"If you get to the top," Johnson said, "put it up."

Lou Lowery

Mount Suribachi
February 23, 9:50 a.m.

Lou Lowery trudged up the last section of the mountainside with the men of Easy Company. Unlike Joe Rosenthal, he was no civilian. Lowery was a seasoned Marine combat photographer. He was also photographic director for the Marine Corps' *Leatherneck* magazine. Lowery had photographed six campaigns in the war, more than any other Marine photographer.

Lowery, along with the other Marines, had expected the march up Suribachi to be a grim one, hampered by enemy fire. But to his surprise, they

One of Lou Lowery's photographs from Mount Suribachi showed a U.S. soldier named Charles Lindberg armed with a flamethrower.

met no resistance. Where were the Japanese? Had they given up the fight? Or were they waiting at the top to bombard them with mortars and grenades?

When the Americans reached the summit with its gaping crater, there was still no sign of the enemy. The men were overjoyed, and First

Lieutenant Schrier sent a group to find something to serve as a pole to raise the U.S. flag the colonel had given them. The men came back with a length of metal pipe the Japanese had apparently used for a rain-catching system.

As Lowery prepared his camera for the flag-raising, one soldier carefully laced the flag through a hole in the pipe. Then four men raised the flag, while Lowry captured the historic moment with his camera. Other soldiers stood guard with rifles in case of an attack.

U.S. soldiers prepared to raise a flag on Mount Suribachi as fighting raged elsewhere on the island.

Lowery's spirits were soaring as he clicked away. They had taken the most strategic point on Iwo Jima without firing a shot. He hoped the hard-fought battle for the island was nearly over.

But a group of Japanese soldiers suddenly burst from a nearby cave and started firing. One hurled a grenade in Lowery's direction. The photographer jumped and tumbled down about 50 feet (15 m) into the volcano's crater. He saved himself by clutching a bush inside the crater. He was not hurt, but his camera was broken.

Climbing out of the crater, Lowery frantically checked his equipment and breathed a sigh of relief. The film inside was safe and intact.

General Holland Smith

Landing craft off Iwo Jima
February 23, 10:45 a.m.

General Smith smiled at Secretary of the Navy James Forrestal. But inside he was fuming.

Smith had been responsible for the secretary's safety ever since he had arrived on board the flagship *Eldorado*. And when Forrestal expressed

U.S. Secretary of the Navy James Forrestal on Iwo Jima

his desire to land on the island, Smith did his best to talk him out of it. He insisted it was too dangerous. But the secretary persisted, and here they were just minutes from landing on the beach. If anything should happen to Forrestal, Smith knew he would bear the blame.

As they drew closer to the beach, the two men looked up and saw the U.S. flag flying on Suribachi.

"Holland," Forrestal said, "the raising of that flag on Mount Suribachi means a Marine Corps for the next five hundred years."

Smith wholeheartedly agreed. Then Forrestal said that when the flag came down, he would like to keep it as a souvenir. Smith did not think that would go well with the top Marine commanders. They would want that flag to remain with the Marines, not with the Navy or U.S. government. But he said nothing as the boat landed on the beach.

Corporal Woody Williams

Corporal Williams hunched down in the shell crater. He and the other Marines crouched in the hole listened intently to their commander, Captain Donald Beck. The captain was telling them that they needed to help the tanks get through the maze of enemy pillboxes safely and move inland. Knowing Williams had trained with flamethrowers, he turned to him and asked if he could help.

"I'll try," said Williams.

Williams grabbed a 70-pound (32-kg) flamethrower, fueled with a lethal blend of gasoline and diesel fuel. While four soldiers with rifles covered him, Williams moved forward. He fired into the thin slot of the first pillbox he reached. He could not hear the cries of the enemy inside, but he imagined their agony. They were either immediately burned to death by the flames or suffocated by the smoke rising from the fire.

Williams continued to move forward, from shell crater to crater. He fired into pillbox after pillbox until his weapon was emptied. Then he fell back behind the lines to get a new, fully filled flamethrower and continued on his dangerous mission.

Joe Rosenthal

Iwo Jima beach
February 23, 11 a.m.

Photographer Rosenthal was having a rough morning. Earlier, while climbing from the command ship to a landing craft, he had slipped on the rope ladder and tumbled into the water. He was nearly crushed between the two vessels. He was soaked, but his camera remained dry in a waterproof bag.

Once on land, Rosenthal managed to photograph Secretary Forrestal and General Smith. Then he caught up with two Marine photographers on the beach. He told them he wanted to climb Suribachi to shoot the flag-raising.

"I think we'll be too late for the flag-raising," one of them told him.

Rosenthal was disappointed but undaunted.

"I'd still like to go up," he told them. They seemed reluctant to join him.

"C'mon, you guys have rifles and I can't carry a weapon," he said. They finally agreed and joined him on the long hike up the mountain.

Lieutenant Colonel Chandler Johnson

Command post
February 23, 11:20 a.m.

All around Lieutenant Colonel Johnson, Marines were cheering, shouting, and even crying at the sight of the U.S. flag atop Suribachi.

"The flag's up! The flag's up!" one soldier yelled.

Johnson was just as moved by the sight of the flag as they were, but he was not about to give in to his emotions. After all, he was a leader and had to set an example of strength to his men. Besides that, his pride was tempered with anger.

Johnson had received word that the Navy secretary wanted the flag as a souvenir. That was

Lou Lowery's photograph showed the small American flag that first waved over Iwo Jima.

something Johnson would not allow. That flag was earned by the blood of the Marines of the battalion, and it would stay with the battalion.

Johnson sent Lieutenant Ted Tuttle, his assistant operations officer, down to the beach. He was supposed to find a replacement flag to raise so the original flag could be lowered and brought to him.

Then, as an afterthought, he called out to Tuttle, "And make it a bigger one."

Private Ira Hayes

Mount Suribachi
February 23, noon

Private Hayes was exhausted. He, his squad leader, and two other members of his rifle squad had just reached the top of Suribachi. Accompanying them was René Gagnon, a runner, who was carrying the second flag and some radio batteries. Hayes and the others were carrying a reel of telephone wire they unrolled all the way up the mountain. The wire would allow the Marines on top to speak directly with the top brass below.

As they arrived, men unfolded the flag Gagnon was carrying. It was the largest flag Hayes had seen since leaving the United States. It was easily twice the size of the first flag that waved briskly in the wind just a short distance away.

Hayes looked forward to resting atop the mountain and enjoying the view below. But it was not to be. An officer ordered him and another Marine to go find a length of pipe that could be used to raise the second flag.

Joe Rosenthal

Mount Suribachi
February 23, 12:10 p.m.

Rosenthal was pleased to see that while he had missed one flag-raising, he was about to witness another. As he looked around at the vista below, two soldiers dragged a heavy piece of drainage pipe to where men were holding the new flag.

The photographer realized that he only had about a minute to plan his strategy for taking a picture of the flag-raising. One of the Marine photographers was setting up his camera to take in both flags. But Rosenthal quickly decided to focus only on the new flag.

Standing only 5 feet 5 inches (1.7 m) tall, Rosenthal knew he would have to get some added height to get a good picture. He quickly tossed some stones together and laid down a few sandbags on top of them. He stood on the makeshift mount, which raised him about a foot and a half off the ground. Then he looked through his viewfinder.

Private Ira Hayes

Mount Suribachi
February 23, 12:11 p.m.

Private Hayes had not intended to join in the flag-raising, but he could see the four men, including René Gagnon, struggling with the pipe pole. He knew it was heavy from carrying it here. It had to weigh at least 100 pounds (45 kg). And the strong wind was not helping to make their job any easier. Hayes grabbed hold from behind the others. A sixth man also jumped in to help.

Joe Rosenthal

Mount Suribachi
February 23, 12:12 p.m.

The men were struggling to raise the pole as the unfurled flag flapped against an iron-gray sky. Rosenthal thought the scene had the three-dimensional strength of a sculpture. Then he took the photo. He looked around him. The only ones paying any attention to the photo op were the three photographers, one of whom was filming it with a movie camera. Everyone else was more focused on the surrounding tunnels and caves out of which Japanese soldiers could come attacking at any moment.

Private Ira Hayes

Mount Suribachi
February 23, 12:14 p.m.

The flag was up, but not yet freestanding. Hayes and two of the others pushed the pole into the soft ground with their body weight. Then they

Joe Rosenthal snapped a photo of the raising of the second flag on Mount Suribachi, and his image became one of the most famous of World War II.

gathered some rocks and ropes to secure it. That is when Hayes turned and noticed the photographers. He remembered his Indian blanket was hanging out of his military belt. He hoped no one would identify him in the picture because of it. He preferred to stay anonymous.

Joe Rosenthal

Mount Suribachi
February 23, 12:15 p.m.

Joe Rosenthal had his photo, but he wanted to take a few more pictures.

"C'mon, fellas," he said, gesturing to the flag. "Gather around."

The Marines followed his direction and crowded around the flag for a group picture. They smiled at the camera, waving their helmets and rifles. It reminded Rosenthal of a high school reunion.

U.S. Marines of the 28th Regiment, Fifth Division, gathered around the flag on Mount Suribachi, raised their rifles, and cheered while posing for photographer Joe Rosenthal.

Corporal Woody Williams

Somewhere beyond Suribachi
February 23, 12:20 p.m.

Corporal Williams took out pillbox after pillbox with his flamethrower. The Japanese were fighting back. One enemy soldier fired at him with a machine gun, the bullets ricocheting off his flamethrower.

When it was too dangerous to get close to a pillbox, Williams tossed a satchel charge through the air. It blew the pillbox to pieces.

At another pillbox, the soldiers inside came out running at Williams with rifles and bayonets. He aimed the flamethrower directly at them. The flames enveloped them where they stood. Williams continued firing into the pillboxes and dodging enemy fire for nearly three more hours.

General Holland Smith

The beach
February 23, 12:30 p.m.

Much to General Smith's concern, Secretary Forrestal was thoroughly enjoying his time on Iwo Jima. Marines crowded around the secretary, eager to shake his hand and exchange a few words.

Smith could hear the gunfire and exploding shells over their chattering. He was fearful that the crowd around them would draw the direct fire of the enemy.

After an hour, Forrestal finally was ready to leave. With a sigh of relief, Smith accompanied him back on board the landing craft. Smith looked again at the now huge flag waving over the mountain. He had heard from a soldier that it came from Pearl Harbor in Hawaii. It seemed appropriate that a flag from the place that brought the United States into the war should now fly over Japanese territory. It seemed to Smith a fitting revenge.

Captain Samaji Inouye

Northern command post, Iwo Jima
February 23, late afternoon

Captain Samaji Inouye, commander of the Japanese Naval Ground Force, waited impatiently for word of the fighting in the south. He was not a man to sit quietly when a battle was raging. Like his commander, General Kuribayashi, Inouye was a skilled samurai swordsman and exhibited great courage. But that is where the resemblance stopped. Inouye was a boaster, always telling his men how great a fighter and partygoer he was.

While Kuribayashi was cool and calm under pressure, Inouye was impulsive and had an explosive temper.

Suddenly a young naval lieutenant, badly wounded, stumbled into the post. Barely able to contain his tears, he told the captain that Suribachi had fallen to the Americans. Inouye's shock quickly turned to anger. This soldier should have died with his comrades on the mountain, not fled to the post with this bad news.

"Shame on you to come here!" Inouye cried. "Shame, shame, shame! You are a coward and a deserter!"

The captain seized his samurai sword and the lieutenant knelt at his feet. He was ready to accept his final punishment. Before he could strike down the man, Inouye felt hands pulling him back. It was his aides. They seized the sword from his grip. Inouye turned away and began to sob uncontrollably.

"Suribachi has fallen," he cried. "Suribachi has fallen."

Joe Rosenthal

On board the *Eldorado*
February 23, 5 p.m.

Rosenthal wasted no time in climbing down Suribachi and rushing back to the command ship. He readied his undeveloped film for the military press center on Guam, where it would be processed. He wrote the caption for his first photo of the second flag raising: "Atop 550-ft. Suribachi Yama, the volcano at the southwest tip of Iwo Jima, Marines of the 2nd Battalion, 28 Regiment, Fifth Division, hoist the Stars and Stripes, signaling the capture of this key position."

Rosenthal thought there was a good chance the flag-raising photo would appear in at least a few stateside newspapers.

Joe Rosenthal stood on Mount Suribachi, with scores of U.S. ships at sea and landing craft on the beach below.

The battle for Iwo Jima stretched on longer than leaders for either side expected.

"I'M NOT GOING BACK"

Captain Severance read his orders with decidedly mixed feelings. Since Easy Company had taken Suribachi, his men had enjoyed a well-earned rest. The battle had moved to the north. A week earlier, Marines had taken the island's central region and its two airfields. But the Japanese were far from beaten and for the past three nights had bombarded the south. Fortunately, in all that time only one of his soldiers had been wounded.

Now the company was being ordered to move north and relieve the 27th Marines. It would be good for the men to be back in action. But it would also mean more of them would be wounded or die. How many more of his men's lives would be lost before the island was theirs?

Lieutenant Colonel Chandler Johnson

The front line
March 2, 2 p.m.

Lieutenant Colonel Johnson was not an officer to stay safely behind the front lines. He visited the battlefront often, talking with the men and seeing what they needed. He knew many of them by name. Now he was walking among the soldiers of Easy Company. He congratulated them on taking a strategic ridge.

As he walked, Johnson came to a shell crater. He expected to see live Marines sheltered inside, but as he drew closer he saw two dead Japanese soldiers lying in the crater. He stepped back in surprise, which caused one Marine standing nearby to laugh. At that moment, a large shell fell at Johnson's feet and exploded. The colonel was instantly blown to pieces.

Colonel Baron Takeichi Nishi

Command post, Cushman's Pocket
March 3, late morning

Baron Nishi wiped the sweat from his forehead with his white scarf and stared at the dim lamp that lit his small room. His command post, a three-level cave complex, was hot and stuffy. There was no air circulation. The passageway leading to the top level had 50 blankets hanging from its ceiling. Nishi had them hung with the hope of holding back the scorching heat if the cave came under a flamethrower attack.

Once a bustling command center filled with soldiers, his cave was now a holding place for the wounded from the battlefront. Nishi knew in his heart that their days were numbered. Most of his men—good, loyal patriots—knew this was their fate and accepted it. They remained faithful to the Bushido code of honor that demanded blind loyalty to the emperor and an honorable death.

But the baron was an educated man who had traveled the world. He knew better. He saw that the

Japanese were in a losing war and that their deaths on this godforsaken island were meaningless. Yet he had to go through the motions. He was just as trapped by his society's expectations as his men were. There was no other way.

General Holland Smith

Marine command post
March 6, midafternoon

General Smith reviewed his troops as they prepared to go forth once more into battle. He put up a front of complete confidence, but inside he was feeling much less sure.

It had been more than a week and a half since Easy Company had taken Suribachi, and the battle for Iwo Jima was far from over. The Japanese held on tenaciously to their underground fortresses of tunnels, caves, and pillboxes. The Marines had to burn, shoot, or bomb them out of their positions, one by one. And that meant a high rate of casualties on both sides.

Smith knew one man was responsible for the strategy—General Kuribayashi. In all his time in the Pacific, Smith had never come up against a more resourceful adversary. He believed that in the end, the Marines would be the victors. But at what terrible price?

After returning to his headquarters, the general shared his respect for Kuribayashi with one of his aides.

"Let's hope the Japanese don't have any more like him!" exclaimed the aide.

Three Japanese soldiers surrendered to a U.S. soldier. Only a fraction of the Japanese men on Iwo Jima were captured alive. Most died in action.

Corporal Woody Williams

Corporal Williams was firing from his foxhole when he was hit. A piece of shrapnel struck him just above his left knee. If the foxhole had been deeper and he had been able to fit his whole body in it, he might have escaped injury.

A corpsman came quickly to his aid. He removed the shrapnel, bandaged the wound, and gave him morphine for the pain.

"I'm going to write a ticket and get you safely back," the corpsman told Williams. Men would come and take the corporal out of the battle.

Williams stared at him. "I'm not going back," he said.

The corpsman persisted. "Well, I put a ticket on you, you have to go back."

The corporal was just as determined to stay where he was. "You better take it off me, or I'll just tear it off," he said. "I'm not going."

The corpsman shook his head in frustration. "OK," he replied sharply. "If you're that stupid." He left and Williams crawled out of the foxhole, clutching his flamethrower in both hands.

Norma Harrison

Airfield, Iwo Jima
March 7, late morning

Twenty-four-year-old Navy nurse Norma Harrison knew she would have her work cut out for her. She was a specialist in combat wounds

Navy flight nurse Jane Kendiegh tends to a wounded marine at the airstrip on Iwo Jima.

and thought she had seen the worst in her war experience. But nothing prepared her for the terrible wounds borne by the injured soldiers on Iwo Jima.

Soon after her plane landed on the airstrip, she was taken to a huge tent. Here the wounded lay helpless on rows of stretchers.

With no doctors present, Harrison and the other nurses began to carry the men on their stretchers onto the airplane. Here they would treat them and then fly with them to stateside hospitals.

A corpsman was with Harrison as she went from soldier to soldier on the plane. One soldier who was severely wounded died as they stood over him. The corpsman began to pull a sheet up over the dead man when Harrison stopped him. She told him to leave him alone. The other men had not noticed he was dead, she explained. They would leave it like that until the plane landed. The corpsman nodded and continued on their rounds.

Captain Samaji Inouye

Command post
March 8, late evening

The time for hiding from the Americans had ended, Captain Inouye decided. He had only a thousand men left under his command, and he was

General Sadasue Senda joined Captain Samaji Inouye in plotting a final assault on U.S. troops.

ready to lead them in a final assault. The plan was to break through the U.S. lines, head south, and retake Mount Suribachi.

Inouye and his fellow commander, General Sadasue Senda, had radioed their plan to General Kuribayashi. He immediately radioed back, "Cancel your banzai charge."

The two leaders ignored the command. Their men were ready to go, armed with rifles, a few machine guns, bamboo spears, and grenades.

Inouye had the officers pass out grenades to the wounded who would be left behind. He also asked the officers to tell the wounded to kill themselves with the grenades when the Americans attacked the cave. Inouye noted, however, that the officers did not have the heart to tell them that.

Inouye let it go. Whether they killed themselves or died fighting, it would be an honorable death.

Wishing well to those left behind, Inouye and Senda led the others out into the darkness.

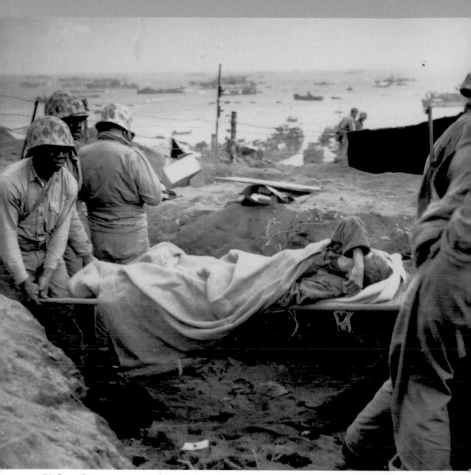

U.S. military personnel carry a malnourished Japanese soldier being evacuated from the island and sent for medical treatment.

U.S. Marines used flamethrowers to strike at enemy soldiers hidden out of sight in caves, tunnels, and pillboxes.

"EVEN THE GODS WOULD WEEP"

General Holland Smith

General Smith stood ramrod straight alongside the other officers as a flag was raised at headquarters in a solemn ceremony. It, like the raising of the two flags on Suribachi, was not a victory rite, but a symbolic one. The ceremony was in part honoring the thousands of Marines who had already died in the prolonged battle. Mortar fire in the near distance shook the flagpole as the flag rose. It was a reminder that the battle was not yet over.

Smith was not a man to show his emotions easily. Yet as he gazed up at the flag, whipping in the wind, he could not hold back the tears. As if to offer an apology for crying, he turned to one of his aides and whispered, "This was the toughest yet." His "yet" did not refer only to the fighting so far in Battle of Iwo Jima or in the war in the Pacific, but to all of Marine Corps history. The aide, also trying to stifle tears, nodded in agreement.

General Tadamichi Kuribayashi

Blockhouse near Kitano Point
March 14, 1945, 1:15 p.m.

General Kuribayashi knew time was running out, but that did not make facing defeat any easier. He and his men had, however, achieved his goal of delaying the U.S. victory, and for that he was grateful. Four days earlier, the Marines had broken through the defenses on the east coast and advanced through the central part of the island.

Now he and nearly all his surviving troops were holed up on the northeast coastal area near Kitano Point. Captain Inouye's banzai attack had been a complete disaster. He and nearly all his men were cut down by the Americans long before they could

General Tadamichi Kuribayashi on Iwo Jima

reach Mount Suribachi. The fool had disobeyed
Kuribayashi's orders and paid the price for it.

The general glanced at the clock. It was time for the broadcast he had been waiting for. He flicked on the radio. An announcer introduced a chorus of Tokyo schoolchildren who began to sing "The Song of Iwo Jima," a number dedicated to Kuribayashi and his surviving troops. The lyrics were:

"Where dark tides billow on the ocean, / A wink-shaped isle of mighty fame /

Guards the gateway to our empire: / Iwo Jima is its name. . ."

Tears came to the general's eyes as he listened. When the song ended, the children recited a prayer for their victory. He said his own silent prayer that his men, hearing the program, would be inspired to persevere. It would not be for victory, but an honorable defeat.

Captain Dave Severance

Command post
March 17, 1945, midmorning

The burden of command weighed heavily on Captain Severance, but he tried not to show it. That morning he received word of the death of Second

Lieutenant Robert Schuelzky. He had been the only other officer in Easy Company still alive. Now Severance was the last surviving officer. Most of the platoons were now led by sergeants. Severance was sure they felt the pressure of command even more than he did. The battle was winding down. In a matter of days, the last pocket of Japanese resistance would be wiped out. But in the meantime, Marines would continue to fight and die.

The newspaper Severance looked at again on his desk that morning raised his spirits. He had saved it since it had arrived some weeks earlier from the United States. Splashed across the front page was the photograph Joe Rosenthal had taken of the six men of Easy Company raising the second flag on Suribachi. It was a beautiful image that Severance felt captured the determination and sacrifice of U.S. soldiers. Apparently millions of other Americans felt the same way. The captain had heard that the photo had already appeared in more than 200 newspapers in the U.S. and around the world. But even here there was a downside. Of the six soldiers in the picture, three of them had been added to the list of the dead.

Norma Harrison

Nurse Harrison felt nothing but the highest respect for the injured soldiers she was attending. Their wounds in many cases were serious. It was all she could do to take away some of the pain they were experiencing. But as hurt as they were, their spirits remained unbeaten.

The men appreciated her nursing skills. But they also appreciated being in the company of a woman. Many had not seen an American woman in many months. As she made her rounds preparing the men for the airplane they would soon be on, one baby-faced soldier tugged at her starched sleeve.

"Nurse, do you have any lipstick?" he asked shyly.

Harrison was startled by the question. "Yes," she replied.

The soldier's face broke into a grin. "Would you please put some on?" he asked. "I'd like to see a woman put lipstick on."

All right," she said and took out a tube of lipstick and rubbed it against her lips.

The soldier's smile widened. "Thank you so much," he said.

She patted his shoulder and moved on down the row of stretchers.

General Tadamichi Kuribayashi

Blockhouse near Kitano Point
March 17, 1945, midafternoon

General Kuribayashi was once again on the move, perhaps for the last time. He knew the Marines would be closing in on his command center soon. He was ready to lead about 1,500 of his remaining men to a remote cave system on the Gorge of Kitano Point. Unlike Captain Inouye, he would not lead a senseless banzai attack, but rather settle in the caves for a last stand. The previous night he had radioed his superiors in Tokyo with this message: "The battle is approaching its end. Since the enemy's landing, even the gods would weep at the bravery of the officers and men under my command."

Colonel Baron Takeichi Nishi

Command post, Cushman's Pocket
March 18, 1945, early evening

Like his commander, Baron Nishi was about to move out from his command post with his remaining men. But there was no safe sanctuary for him to flee to. Two days before, the Third Division of Marines had fired on the entrance to his complex as they passed by. The fire from the guns and flamethrowers had burned his eyes. It had left him practically blind. The once-proud Olympic horseman now had to be led around by his adjutant.

Before leaving the compound, Nishi ordered that the soldiers who were too wounded and weak to move be given pistols, grenades, and a three-day supply of bread. Then, holding the hand of his adjutant, he led the men out into the night to their meeting with destiny.

U.S. soldiers with a prisoner near the mouth of one the caves that honeycombed Iwo Jima

General Tadamichi Kuribayashi

Gorge of Kitano Point
March 22, 1945, late afternoon

The end was near and General Kuribayashi approached it with the philosophical calm of a true samurai. He had received word that the blockhouse had been blown up by the Americans. Nearly all his

89

men were dead. With the Marines closing in, he sent his last radio dispatch to Tokyo.

"We are still fighting," he said. "The strength under my command is now about 400. Tanks are attacking us. The enemy suggested we surrender through a loudspeaker, but our officers and men just laughed and paid no attention."

Nearly a week earlier, Kuribayashi had sent a poem he wrote in a telegram to his superiors. It showed the artistic, sensitive side of this warrior. The poem read in part: "Unable to complete this heavy task for our country / Arrows and bullets all spent, so sad we fall."

Captain Dave Severance

Command post
March 23, 1945, early afternoon

If anything had kept Captain Severance's hopes up so far from home, it was his wife's pregnancy back in the States. But those hopes were dashed when he received a letter from home. It said she had delivered a baby boy, but that the infant had died soon after birth. Severance was devastated.

There was another man named Dave, David Bowman, a corporal in Easy Company. His wife was also about to have a baby. Severance was happy for Bowman, who was about to be relieved with his platoon. The captain rushed to the front as the new troops arrived. With any luck, Bowman would

The landscape of the island was laid to waste by bombs, mortar rounds, flamethrowers, and every other weapon U.S. fighting forces had at their disposal.

not have to come back to fight another day. As Severance stood nearby, Bowman informed the new platoon leader about the area. Suddenly an enemy bullet hit Bowman. He died almost instantly.

Severance returned to his command post, a shattered man. In the incoming mail he saw a letter

U.S. soldiers inspect the remains of a hidden Japanese defense.

for Bowman from his wife. It was more than he could bear. This man, who was a tower of strength to his men, went off by himself and cried. When he was composed again, he returned to the post and went back to work.

Corporal Woody Williams

Near the beach
March 24, 1945, late morning

Resourceful Corporal Williams had just been given his last mission by his commanding officer. A captured Japanese soldier had told them 300 Japanese troops were holed up in a nearby cave on a hillside near the ocean. They were among the last enemy holdouts. It was Williams's job to seal off the cave, entombing the men inside.

Williams crept up to the cave's entrance, hauling two 8-pound (3.6-kg) bags of explosives. He lit a 10-second fuse on one of the bags and tossed it into the opening. Then he ran for the beach.

Six seconds passed. Eight. Ten. The only sound he heard was a soft pop. Perhaps the fuse cap was damp and did not go off.

Williams tried the second bag. Again, no explosion.

The commanding officer sent him to headquarters for a new box of caps. He returned with the caps and a third bag. He tossed it into the cave with a new fuse. The charge not only went off, but set off the other two bags. The explosion was so powerful that it literally tore the hillside off the mountain. The cave was completely sealed off.

His commanding officer praised him for a job well done. But Williams expressed his sadness for the men trapped inside the cave. The officer responded that the prisoner could have been lying or not have known if the men were in there. Williams agreed that it was better that they did not know the truth.

Captain Dave Severance

Troop transport ship off Iwo Jima
March 26, 1945, early evening

It was over at last. The final, desperate attack from the few remaining Japanese soldiers had taken place that morning at the northernmost airfield.

Whatever Japanese men were still hidden on the island were offering no resistance. The battle was won. Now the men of Easy Company were leaving with their captain. A small boat brought them to a transport ship. Some of the men were so weak that the ship's crew members had to pull them over the rail onto the deck.

Soldiers gather around as one of the enemy survivors is led away.

Captain Severance exulted in his first hot shower in weeks. He felt like a new man in fresh, clean clothes. The food in the mess hall was delicious and there was plenty of it. But Severance's stomach had shrunk and he could not eat much.

Marines injured in the fighting on Iwo Jima await evacuation from the island.

He fell asleep almost as soon as his head hit the pillow on a bunk below deck. But a noise awakened him in the middle of the night and he forgot where he was. Thinking he was back on the island in the middle of a battle, he jumped up. He hit his head on the bunk above.

In the morning, Severance shared the experience with another soldier over breakfast. The Marine smiled sheepishly. He said the same thing happened to him and he had a bump on his head to prove it.

For perhaps the first time in a long time, Dave Severance joined in the laughter of everyone at the table. It felt good to laugh. It felt good to be alive.

EPILOGUE

When General Holland Smith said, "This was the toughest yet" about Iwo Jima, his words were truer than he could have imagined. A total of 6,821 Americans, most of them Marines, died on Iwo Jima during the 36-day battle. Total casualties, including the wounded, were 26,038. It was the bloodiest battle

The price of victory was steep, as U.S. casualties on Iwo Jima numbered in the thousands.

in Marine Corps history. On the Japanese side, nearly all of the 21,000 soldiers on Iwo Jima died, with fewer than 1,000 prisoners taken alive.

Of the 82 Congressional Medals of Honor awarded to Marines during World War II, 27 of them—one third—were earned on Iwo Jima. More medals were given for action in that battle than in any battle in any war in which Americans have fought.

The sacrifices and heroism of the Marines on Iwo Jima were not in vain. Over the remaining five months of the war, U.S. fighter planes made a total of 2,251 air landings on the island's two airfields. Many of these aircraft and their crews would have been lost in the Pacific if it were not for Iwo Jima. The island played a central role in the continuing air attacks on Japan.

Then on August 6, 1945, the U.S. bomber Enola Gay flew over Iwo Jima on its way to drop an atom bomb on the Japanese city of Hiroshima. Days after a second bomb was dropped on the city of Nagasaki, Japan surrendered unconditionally. The long war came to an end.

The U.S. occupied Iwo Jima until 1968, when it was returned to Japan. Today, Iwo Jima is a national shrine to the thousands of Japanese soldiers whose bones still lie entombed in its sealed caves and tunnels. Their exact number remains unknown. Only family members of these war dead are permitted to visit the island. U.S. military veterans and other Americans can visit the island during an annual organized tour.

On February 19, 1985, the 40th anniversary of the battle was observed. A "Reunion of Honor" was held with both U.S. and Japanese veterans attending.

As for those among the dead, the bodies of General Kuribayashi and Baron Nishi were never recovered. How they met their ends remains a matter of speculation. Kuribayashi is said to have committed ritual suicide with the help of his aides in a cave near Kitano Point on March 23, 1945, although there is no solid evidence of this.

After he led his men into a desperate battle during the night of March 18, 1945, Baron Nishi is thought to have gathered his surviving fighters in several caves near the beach. The next day, some

Photographer Lou Lowery captured an image showing both flags placed on Mount Suribachi early in the fighting.

say, looking toward the ocean, he shot himself with a pistol. What is known for certain is that back in Japan, his beloved horse, Uranus, died a week later.

Lou Lowery's photographs of the first flag-raising on Suribachi did not appear in print until 1947. They never became as famous as Joe Rosenthal's iconic photo of the second flag-raising. Lowery died in 1987 at age 70. He was buried in Quantico National Cemetery in Prince William County, Virginia. His grave ironically is not far from the Marine Corps War Memorial, based on Rosenthal's photo. That photograph won the Pulitzer Prize in 1945 and became the most famous image of the war in the United States. It was made the central theme of the Seventh War Bond Tour and helped raise $2.4 billion for the war effort. That was more money made than from any other bond tour.

Rosenthal made only $6,000 from newspaper bonuses and prize money for his famous photo. After the war he worked as a photographer for the *San Francisco Chronicle*. He retired in 1986 and was named an honorary Marine in 1996. Rosenthal died 10 years later at age 94.

Ira Hayes, one of the three surviving flag-raisers in Rosenthal's photo, was enlisted to accompany the war bond tour. A humble, shy man, he never felt comfortable as a media star and war hero. He insisted that the real heroes had died on Iwo Jima.

After the war President Harry Truman presented Woody Williams with the Medal of Honor for his actions on Iwo Jima.

After leaving the Marines, Hayes's life took a sad downward spiral. He drank to drown his sorrow and feelings of guilt and was arrested numerous times for disorderly conduct. A social worker who tried to help Hayes claimed, "His attitude was not bitterness, but some hurt that I couldn't sort out."

On a cold morning in January 1955, nearly 10 years after the flag-raising that made him famous, Hayes was found dead from overexposure and alcohol poisoning. He was 32 years old.

Norma Harrison continued to help heal wounded and sick soldiers and sailors after Iwo Jima. Woody Williams was awarded the Congressional Medal of Honor by President Harry Truman on October 5, 1945, for his acts of heroism on Iwo Jima. He retired from the Marine Corps Reserves in 1969 and served for 35 years as a chaplain of the Congressional Medal of Honor Society.

Holland Smith returned to the United States in July 1945 to head the Marine Training and Replacement Command at Camp Pendleton, California. He retired from the Marines with the rank of lieutenant general in 1946 at age 64. Smith settled in La Jolla, California, where he spent much of his time gardening. He died in 1967 after a long illness. His son John Smith was a rear admiral in the Navy. The Marine Corps base on Oahu, Hawaii, is named Camp Smith in Holland's honor.

Dave Severance went on to be a Marine fighter pilot in the Korean War (1950–1953). He flew 62 missions in Korea and was awarded the Distinguished Flying Cross and four Air Medals. He retired from the Marines with the rank of colonel in 1968. Since then Severance has been active in contacting Easy Company veterans from Iwo Jima. He has published a newspaper for them and organized several reunions.

The three surviving men from Joe Rosenthal's famous photograph later raised a flag together in a Washington, D.C., ceremony.

TIMELINE

JUNE 1944: U.S. air and naval bombardment of Iwo Jima begins in advance of a planned land invasion; General Tadamichi Kuribayashi arrives on Iwo Jima to take over command of its 20,000 soldiers.

FEBRUARY 16, 1945: U.S. naval ships offshore begin the bombardment of Iwo Jima.

FEBRUARY 19, 1945: The land invasion of Iwo Jima by two divisions of Marines begins; a third division arrives later that month.

FEBRUARY 23, 1945: Members of Easy Company take Mount Suribachi on the southern end of the island and plant two U.S. flags on its summit.

FEBRUARY 24–MARCH 10, 1945: The Marines move steadily inland until they have taken over all of the island except for the northeastern corner.

MARCH 2, 1945: Lieutenant Colonel Chandler Johnson, one of the most beloved Marine commanders, is killed by an exploding shell at the front line.

MARCH 7, 1945: A group of U.S. nurses arrives on the island to care for the many wounded soldiers and accompany them on airplanes back stateside.

MARCH 8, 1945: Japanese Captain Samaji Inouye leads a large group of soldiers in a desperate banzai attack on the Americans. Nearly all of them are killed by the Marines.

MARCH 17, 1945: General Kuribayashi abandons his headquarters in the north and moves to a more secluded spot, knowing the end is near.

MARCH 22, 1945: General Kuribayashi radios his last dispatch to Tokyo.

MARCH 24, 1945: Corporal Woody Williams uses explosives to seal off a cave said to contain one of the last groups of Japanese soldiers.

MARCH 25, 1945: The Marines declare victory on Iwo Jima, and the island is made secure.

APRIL 7, 1945: B-29 fighter planes fly the first fighter-escorted missions against Japan, landing on Iwo Jima.

AUGUST 6 AND 9, 1945: The first and second atomic bombs are dropped by U.S. planes on the Japanese cities of Hiroshima and Nagasaki.

AUGUST 14, 1945: Japan surrenders unconditionally.

SEPTEMBER 2, 1945: The formal surrender of Japan takes place on board the battleship USS *Missouri* in Tokyo Bay.

OCTOBER 5, 1945: Woody Williams and 13 other servicemen are presented with the Congressional Medal of Honor by President Harry Truman.

GLOSSARY

adjutant (AJ-uh-tuhnt)—an officer who assists a commanding officer

adversary (AD-vuhr-sere-ee)—opponent, enemy

banzai (BAHN-zeye)—Japanese battle cry when attacking; a frontal charge on an enemy

battalion (buh-TAL-yuhn)—military unit made up of two or more companies, forming part of a regiment

campaign (kam-PAIN)—series of related military operations with a common objective

casualties (KAZH-oo-uhl-tees)—number of soldiers who have been wounded, killed, captured, or missing in action

corpsman (KORZ-man)—soldier trained to give medical assistance to the wounded

division (di-VIZH-uhn)—large, organized military unit made up of infantry, artillery, and supporting groups

equestrian (i-KWES-tree-uhn)—athlete who performs or competes on horseback

flagship (FLAG-ship)—ship carrying the commanding officer of a fleet

foxhole (FOKS-hol)—hole dug in the ground by soldiers to shelter them from enemy fire

iconic (eye-KON-ick)—relating to pictures or images that are highly symbolic

morale (muh-RAL)—condition of a person or group of people with respect to their confidence and positive spirit

platoon (pluh-TOON)—small military unit that is part of a company

propaganda (prop-uh-GAN-duh)—ideas of a group promoted in a biased way to influence others

regiment (REJ-uh-muhnt)—military unit made up of three battalions that forms part of a division

samurai (SAM-oo-ri)—member of a Japanese warrior class, going back to feudal times

satchel charge (SACH-uhl-CHARJ)—explosive on a board fitted with a rope or hook for carrying and attaching to an enemy's position

shrapnel (SHRAP-nahl)—fragments from an exploding shell

siege (SEEJ)—act of surrounding an enemy in a prolonged attack

theater (THEE-uh-tuhr)—place where action takes place; a field of operations in a large war

turret (TUR-it)—revolving, armored structure housing guns and gunners on a tank

CRITICAL THINKING QUESTIONS

1. Why was the tiny island of Iwo Jima so important for the Americans to capture and for the Japanese to hold on to?

2. Both the Japanese and Americans exhibited great courage and skill in the long battle. Can you give one or two examples of individuals on each side who demonstrated this?

3. The photograph of the second flag-raising taken by Joe Rosenthal became an iconic image that captured the nation's imagination as no other war picture did. Look at the photo as shown on page 60. What is it about the photo that made it so powerful? What message did it convey about the Americans fighting the war?

INTERNET SITES

Iwo Jima Facts
www.american-historama.org/1929-1945-depression-ww2-era/iwo-jima.htm

Iwo Jima Facts for Kids
https://kids.kiddle.co/Iwo_Jima

Ten Interesting Facts About the Battle of Iwo Jima
https://learnodo-newtonic.com/battle-of-iwo-jima-facts

World War II: Battle of Iwo Jima
https://www.ducksters.com/history/world_war_ii/battle_of_iwo_jima.php

FURTHER READING

Burgan, Michael. *Raising the Flag: How a Photograph Gave a Nation Hope in Wartime*. North Mankato, MN: Compass Point Books, 2011.

Doeden, Matt. *At Battle in World War II: An Interactive Battlefield Adventure*. North Mankato, MN: Capstone, 2015.

Marsico, Katie. *World War II: Why They Fought*. North Mankato, MN: Capstone, 2016.

Sturgeon, Alison. *World War II: The Definitive Visual History from Blitzkrieg to the Atom Bomb*. New York: DK Publishing, 2015.

SELECTED BIBLIOGRAPHY

Bradley, James. *Flags of Our Fathers*. New York: Bantam Books, 2000.

Buell, Hal. *Uncommon Valor, Common Virtue: Iwo Jima and the Photograph That Captured America*. New York: Berkley Publishing Group, 2006.

Smith, Larry. *Iwo Jima: World War II Veterans Remember the Greatest Battle of the Pacific*. New York: W.W. Norton, 2008.

Sulzberger, C.L. *The American Heritage Picture History of World War II*. Avenel, NJ: Wings Books, 1966.

Wheeler, Richard. *Iwo*. New York: Lippincott and Crowell, 1980.

Wright, Derrick. *Iwo Jima 1945: The Marines Raise the Flag on Mount Suribachi*. Oxford, Eng.: Osprey Publishing, 2004.

INDEX

ABOUT THE AUTHOR

Steven Otfinoski has written more than 200 books for young readers. His previous books in the Tangled History series include *Day of Infamy: Attack on Pearl Harbor* and *Smooth Seas and a Fighting Chance: The Story of the Sinking of Titanic*. Among his many other books for Capstone are the You Choose book *World War II Infantrymen* and *Split History of the Battle of Fort Sumter*. Three of his nonfiction books have been named Books for the Teen Age by the New York Public Library. He lives in Connecticut with his wife and dog.